SWAGGER

BY MARK ROEMHILDT

TORQUE

TM

BELLWETHER MEDIA · MINNEAPOLIS, MN

Are you ready to take it to the extreme?
Torque books thrust you into the action-packed world
of sports, vehicles, mystery, and adventure. These books
may include dirt, smoke, fire, and dangerous stunts.
WARNING : read at your own risk.

Library of Congress Cataloging-in-Publication Data

Roemhildt, Mark.
  Jack Swagger / by Mark Roemhildt.
     p. cm. -- (Torque: pro wrestling champions)
  Includes bibliographical references and index.
  Summary: "Engaging images accompany information about Jack Swagger. The combination of
high-interest subject matter and light text is intended for students in grades 3 through 7"--Provided by
publisher.
  ISBN 978-1-60014-751-7 (hardcover : alk. paper)
  1. Jack Swagger, 1982---Juvenile literature. 2. Wrestlers--United States--Biography--Juvenile literature. I.
Title.
  GV1196.J338R64 2012
  796.812092--dc23
  [B]   2011031242

Printed in the United States of America, North Mankato, MN.

CONTENTS

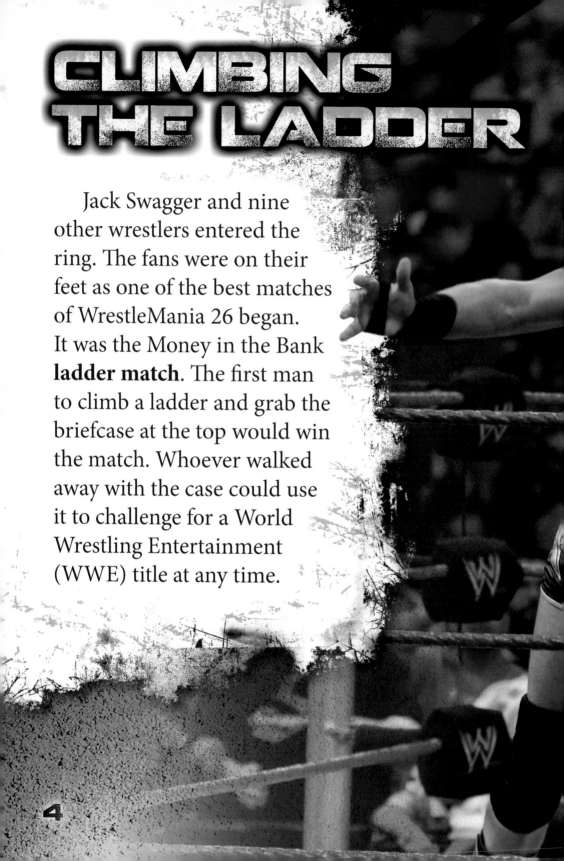

CLIMBING THE LADDER

Jack Swagger and nine other wrestlers entered the ring. The fans were on their feet as one of the best matches of WrestleMania 26 began. It was the Money in the Bank **ladder match**. The first man to climb a ladder and grab the briefcase at the top would win the match. Whoever walked away with the case could use it to challenge for a World Wrestling Entertainment (WWE) title at any time.

One by one, wrestlers were eliminated. Soon only Christian and Swagger remained. Each man climbed up one side of the ladder. Christian reached for the case. Swagger slammed it in his face before he could grab it. Christian flew off the ladder, and Swagger grabbed the case. He had won the match and a chance to wrestle for a WWE Championship!

WHO IS JACK SWAGGER?

QUICK HIT!

WrestleMania 26 was the first time a Money in the Bank ladder match had ever featured ten competitors. Earlier matches had no more than eight.

Donald Jake Hager, Jr. was born on March 24, 1982 in Perry, Oklahoma. People called him Jake. He started wrestling when he was 5 years old. In high school, he won two state wrestling championships and was a football star. The University of Oklahoma gave him a **scholarship** to play football and wrestle.

Jake soon focused on just wrestling. He became one of the best college wrestlers in the country. He was named an **All-American**. In 2006, he set a record with 30 pins in one season. He also met Jim Ross of WWE. Ross encouraged Jake to try professional wrestling.

11

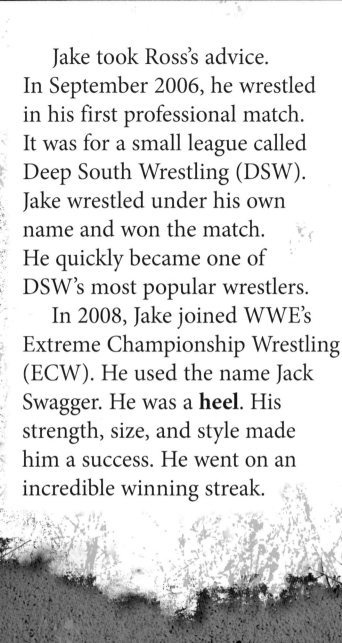

Jake took Ross's advice. In September 2006, he wrestled in his first professional match. It was for a small league called Deep South Wrestling (DSW). Jake wrestled under his own name and won the match. He quickly became one of DSW's most popular wrestlers.

In 2008, Jake joined WWE's Extreme Championship Wrestling (ECW). He used the name Jack Swagger. He was a **heel**. His strength, size, and style made him a success. He went on an incredible winning streak.

QUICK HIT!

Jake made his first television appearance for WWE in 2007. He served as a security guard for WWE star John Cena.

BECOMING A CHAMPION

QUICK HIT!

Swagger gave himself the nickname "the All-American American."

Swagger got his shot at ECW Champion Matt Hardy in January 2009. It was a long match. Swagger won by driving Hardy's head into a **turnbuckle**. He became the new ECW Champion and remained undefeated. His first loss did not come for another month.

Swagger's next big title shot came in March 2010. He used his Money in the Bank case to challenge Chris Jericho for the World Heavyweight Championship. Jericho had just been injured and was no match for Swagger. Swagger won the match and became the new champion.

QUICK HIT!

In 2011, Swagger trained wrestler Michael Cole. He and Cole later formed a tag team.

17

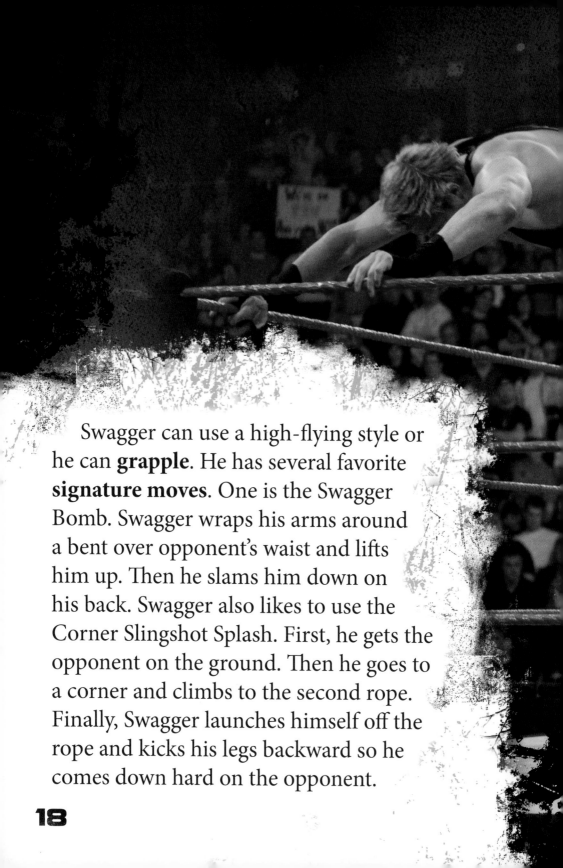

Swagger can use a high-flying style or he can **grapple**. He has several favorite **signature moves**. One is the Swagger Bomb. Swagger wraps his arms around a bent over opponent's waist and lifts him up. Then he slams him down on his back. Swagger also likes to use the Corner Slingshot Splash. First, he gets the opponent on the ground. Then he goes to a corner and climbs to the second rope. Finally, Swagger launches himself off the rope and kicks his legs backward so he comes down hard on the opponent.

CORNER
SLINGSHOT
SPLASH

19

ANKLE
LOCK

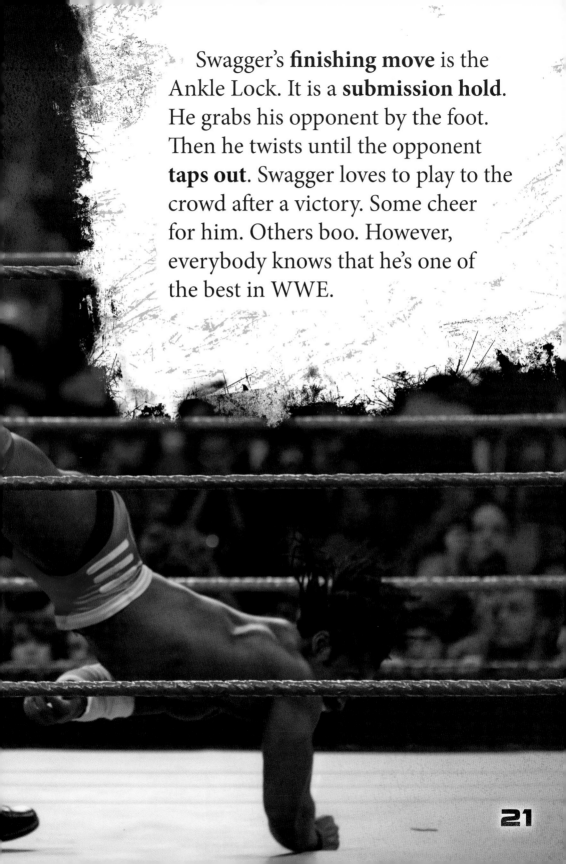

Swagger's **finishing move** is the Ankle Lock. It is a **submission hold**. He grabs his opponent by the foot. Then he twists until the opponent **taps out**. Swagger loves to play to the crowd after a victory. Some cheer for him. Others boo. However, everybody knows that he's one of the best in WWE.

GLOSSARY

All-American—an honor given to a sport's top college competitors

finishing move—a wrestling move meant to finish off an opponent so that he can be pinned

grapple—to maintain physical contact with another wrestler during a fight

heel—a wrestler seen by fans as a villain

ladder match—a wrestling match in which a ladder is placed in the middle of the ring; the first wrestler to reach the object at the top wins the match.

scholarship—money given to a student to pay for school

signature moves—moves that a wrestler is famous for performing

submission hold—a wrestling move that puts an opponent in great pain or risk of injury; submission holds usually cause the opponent to tap out.

taps out—voluntarily ends a match, usually because of pain caused by an opponent's submission hold

turnbuckle—a part of the ring that holds the ropes together; a ring has three turnbuckles in each corner.

TO LEARN MORE

AT THE LIBRARY

Black, Jake. *The Ultimate Guide to WWE*. New York, N.Y.: Grosset & Dunlap, 2010.

Kaelberer, Angie Peterson. *Cool Pro Wrestling Facts*. Mankato, Minn.: Capstone Press, 2011.

Stone, Adam. *John Cena*. Minneapolis, Minn.: Bellwether Media, 2011.

ON THE WEB

Learning more about Jack Swagger is as easy as 1, 2, 3.

1. Go to www.factsurfer.com.

2. Enter "Jack Swagger" into the search box.

3. Click the "Surf" button and you will see a list of related Web sites.

With factsurfer.com, finding more information is just a click away.

INDEX